Checkered Flag!

Contents

Big Ideas 2

Vocabulary 3

Characters 4

Checkered Flag! 5

Wrap Up 21

Glossary 22

Steck Vaughn
A Harcourt Achieve Imprint

www.Steck-Vaughn.com
1-800-531-5015

> Does moving fast scare you or thrill you? My name's Sunita, and I like to race. I've been bike racing for a while. One day, a friend asked me to get behind the wheel. How do you think I did?

> There were a few things to learn about cars. These ideas helped me.

Big Ideas

- Machines, such as cars, televisions, and computers, require energy to work.

- Energy often comes from fossil fuels, such as coal, oil, and natural gas. Fossil fuels are made from decaying plants and animals that died millions of years ago.

- When fossil fuels are burned, they release gases into the air. Some of these gases cause air pollution.

- An object at rest stays at rest until something moves it. An object in motion stays in motion until something stops it. This is called inertia.

- Machines can be modified, or improved, to make them perform better.

Vocabulary

acceleration the rate at which something speeds up
*After a few repairs, the car's **acceleration** improved.*

assemble to put together
*The instructions helped us **assemble** the model airplane.*

motion movement
*The **motion** of the waves was very peaceful.*

prepare to get ready
*The cooking class worked hard to **prepare** the meal for their final exam.*

ratio a comparison between two quantities expressed as one number divided into the other
*The **ratio** of boys to girls in the class is about 2 to 1.*

Characters

Sunita

Jen

Leo

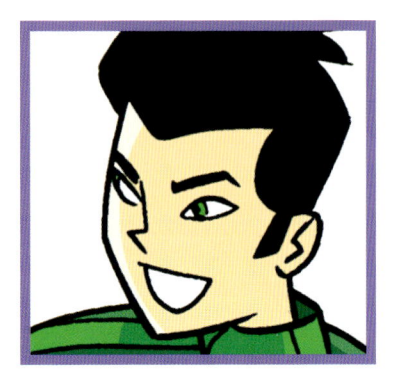

Rex

Alfredo

"Rex is leading!"

"He's going to win."

"Oh no! Rex is spinning out!"

CRASH!

HOOK
EWAY
Rex, are you alright?
I'm alright, just disappointed.
We thought you might be hurt. That was a wipe-out!
Quarter midgets are very safe. They have seat belts, shoulder harnesses, and a *roll cage*.
I was in first place. Then I messed up. Alfredo the Great wins again.

Don't feel bad. Alfredo's got five cars. His dad even owns the track.
Rex, you're not the problem. It's the car.
What do you mean?
It's unstable. You have tiny tires and horrible *weight distribution*. The front-to-back *ratio* is all wrong.
Taking tips from a girl, Rex? You must be desperate.

Alfredo, just leave!
Wait! What are you saying?
Girls don't understand racing. It's too difficult.
You are so wrong.
I am so right.
Alfredo, you've got your trophy. Just go.
I'll prove I'm right. There's car number 8. Here are the keys. Race me once. If you win, it's yours.
You've got it! Just give us three weeks to get ready.
Hey, Rex, you won't be finishing last anymore. The girls will.

A few days later, Sunita visits Jen and her brother Leo.
Nice sculpture, Leo!
Thanks. It's not quite done yet.
You're really going to race, Jen?
No, you are.
Huh?
You race bikes. You're the speed demon.
I like speed that I *generate* with my legs, not with *fossil fuels*.
Fossils? We're talking cars, not dinosaurs.
She means oil and gas. When cars burn fossil fuels, they create gases that *contribute* to *global warming*.

What do you say, Sunita? Should I send this car back to Alfredo?
I don't know.
I guess I could try it once.
IGNITION
ZOOM!
Maybe one race won't heat up the planet too much.

The next afternoon, Jen is ready to get to work.

"Alfredo wouldn't loan me his fastest car. That'd be dumb."

"But we can make it really fast once we *modify* it."

"Let's get rid of the heavy steel panels. We'll *assemble* the body from *fiberglass* instead. That will improve the power-to-weight ratio."

"That means more speed! Plus, we'll save fuel."

"We'll lengthen the *axles* and widen the *wheelbase*. That gives you more stability."

"I won't tip over like Rex did."

OLD
NEW!

"This *spoiler* will also help you zoom around turns."

11

12

Finally, the car is ready! Sunita meets Jen and Leo at the track.

Don't you think it's a little flashy, Leo?

That was the only fiberglass I had.

Who cares about the color? Give me the keys!

ZOOM!

That's serious *acceleration!*

WOW! Our modifications really helped generate some speed.

13

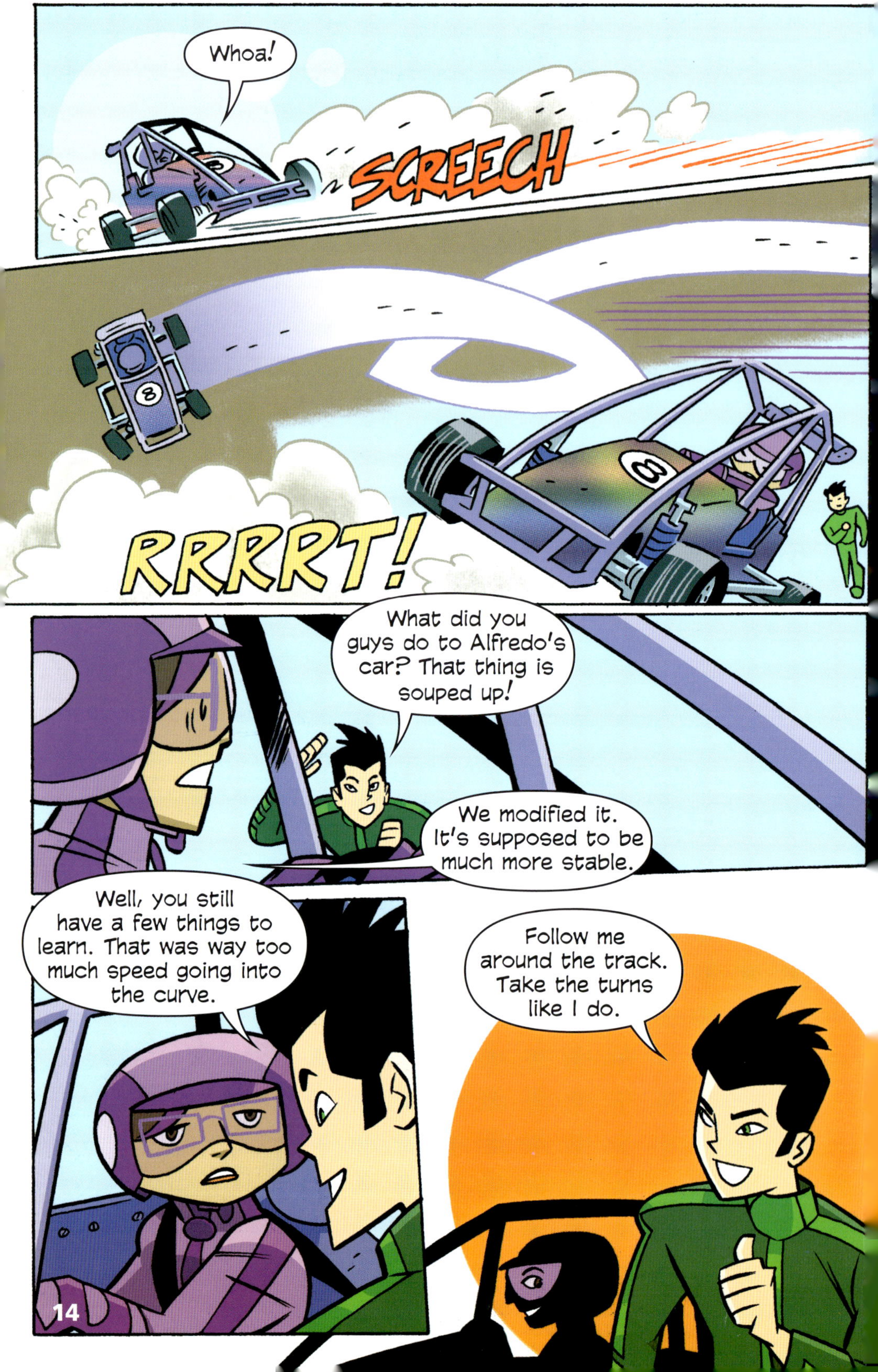
Whoa!
SCREECH
RRRRT!
What did you guys do to Alfredo's car? That thing is souped up!
We modified it. It's supposed to be much more stable.
Well, you still have a few things to learn. That was way too much speed going into the curve.
Follow me around the track. Take the turns like I do.

"That was a nice spin-out. I guess a quarter-midget is too hard to control— for a girl."

"That was her first try. Give her a few laps to get up to speed."

"She's got two more weeks to *prepare*. But it won't help. By the way, that car looks awful, like one of Leo's sculptures."

"Hey, Leo's sculptures win awards!"

"Maybe so, but that car's not going to win any races."

15

These new brakes help me *decelerate* with more control.
SCREECH!
Not bad! After a few laps, you were taking the turns as well as I was!
It's like bike racing. Go fast, but keep it in control.
You did a great job with that car, Jen.
Just wait until race day, Rex. I've got some more tinkering to do.

Two weeks later, it's race day.

What do you think, Leo? Will she do okay?

She'd better. We've been working for weeks. I need to get back to my sculptures!

You know I've got the fastest car here, right?

Only if you still consider this one yours.

Funny.

VOOOM!

VOOOM!

ZOOOM

She's going to win! There's just one lap to go.

Remember what happened to Rex last time? He was leading, too.

I can't let her win. I'll cut her off!

Whoa!

RED HOOK
VOOOOM!
CEWA
RED HOOK
CRASH!
ZOOM!
ZOOM!
RED HOOK
I'll never hear the end of this. At least the roll cage works.
Yes!

That car looks great, Alfredo.
It's like one of my sculptures.
Very funny!
RED
You did it, Sunita. What a race!
We did it together. What a team!
I've got ideas for more improvements.
Jen, we proved our point. Now, I'm going back to bike racing.
What about the car?
Let's give it to Rex. Alfredo needs the competition.
FINISH

Wrap Up

Well, that was fun! I think I'll stick with bikes for a while, though. They're more my speed. Speaking of speed, let's review some of the facts from the story.

- Fossil fuels (such as coal, oil, and natural gas) are made from plants or animals that decayed millions of years ago.
- Gasoline, a product made from fossil fuels, powers most of our cars. The use of fossil fuels increases the amount of carbon dioxide in the air. This could lead to rising temperatures around the planet.
- An object at rest stays at rest until some force moves it. An object in motion stays in motion until some force stops it. This is called inertia.
- Machines can be modified, or improved, to make them perform better.

If you want a serious ride someday, be sure to read *Hot Rods, Lowriders, and Veggie Cars*.

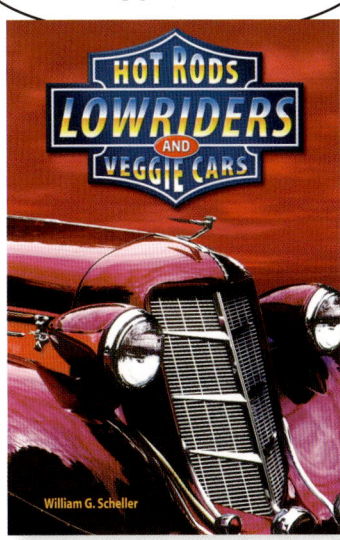

21

Glossary

acceleration (*noun*) the rate at which something speeds up

assemble (*verb*) to put together

axle (*noun*) a rod running through the center of a wheel, on which the wheel turns

contribute (*verb*) to add to; to give something to an existing amount

decelerate (*verb*) to slow down

fiberglass (*noun*) a material made of fine glass fibers, often used to make cars

fossil fuel (*noun*) coal, oil, or natural gas formed from decayed animals and plants

generate (*verb*) to produce something

global warming (*noun*) the gradual rise in the earth's temperature due to the greenhouse effect

modify (*verb*) to change something

motion (*noun*) movement

prepare (*verb*) to get ready

quarter midget (*noun*) a small racing car built for kids

ratio (*noun*) a comparison between two quantities expressed as one number divided into the other

roll cage (*noun*) a protective frame of metal bars used to protect a driver in a car

spoiler (*noun*) a curved, winglike attachment on the back of a car to reduce lift

weight distribution (*noun*) the spreading out of an object's weight over an area

weld (*verb*) to join two pieces of metal together by heating them

wheelbase (*noun*) the distance from the center of the front wheels to the center of the back wheels

Idioms

cut me off (*page 18*) to overtake and move in front of
I stopped suddenly when a big truck cut me off.

souped up (*page 14*) mechanically improved for power or looks
My brother's souped up car is the hottest thing on the road.